Employed To Entrepreneur

Navigating The Transition With
Financial Security & Business
Success

HASSAN AFIFI

Hassan Afifi

EMPLOYED TO ENTREPRENEUR – Navigating The
Transition With Financial Security & Business Success

CONTENTS

INTRODUCTION

In today's ever-evolving business landscape, the dream of entrepreneurship is becoming increasingly attainable. Many individuals aspire to start their own businesses, driven by the desire for independence, creative fulfilment, and financial prosperity. However, the decision to embark on an entrepreneurial journey can be daunting, especially when it comes to maintaining financial stability during the transition from employment to full-time entrepreneurship.

Recognising the advantages of maintaining employment while venturing into entrepreneurship:

One of the key advantages of maintaining employment while venturing into entrepreneurship is the financial security it provides. Having a stable income from your job ensures that you can meet your financial obligations and responsibilities while you establish your business. It allows you to cover personal expenses, pay bills, and handle any unforeseen financial emergencies that may arise during the transition period. By recognising the benefits of remaining employed, you can approach your entrepreneurial journey with a sense of confidence and security.

Embracing a balanced approach for financial security and successful business transition:

A balanced approach is essential for achieving financial security and a successful transition from employment to entrepreneurship. It involves carefully managing both your job and your business responsibilities to minimise financial risks and maintain a steady income stream. By striking a balance between the two, you can ensure that your personal finances remain stable while you focus on building and growing your business.

In this book, we will explore the practical strategies and techniques that will help you embrace this balanced approach. We will guide you through the process of assessing your financial stability, understanding your personal financial obligations and responsibilities, and creating a comprehensive financial plan that ensures stability during the transition. By recognising the advantages of maintaining employment, we will help you leverage your job as a foundation for your entrepreneurial journey, tapping into its resources, network, and expertise.

Moreover, we will delve into the importance of crafting a detailed business plan that aligns with your employment and transition goals. This plan will help you navigate the challenges and mitigate the financial risks associated with starting a business. We will also discuss effective time management strategies for balancing your job and business responsibilities, allowing you to allocate your time efficiently and maximise your productivity.

Additionally, we will address the significance of financial planning and risk management during the transition. You will learn how to create a budget, manage cash flow, and identify potential risks. By implementing suitable risk management strategies, such as insurance coverage and contingency planning, you can navigate the transition period with confidence and minimize any financial setbacks.

By embracing a balanced approach and implementing the strategies outlined in this book, you can confidently navigate the transition from employment to entrepreneurship. You will gain the knowledge and tools necessary to maintain financial security while building a successful business. We will provide practical insights and actionable advice to help you achieve your entrepreneurial goals without compromising your financial stability.

Now, let us embark on this journey together, as we guide you through the transition from being employed to becoming a thriving entrepreneur, all while ensuring financial security and successful business growth.

EMPLOYED TO ENTREPRENEUR – Navigating The
Transition With Financial Security & Business Success

CHAPTER I
ASSESSING YOUR FINANCIAL STABILITY

Before embarking on your entrepreneurial journey, it is crucial to conduct a thorough assessment of your financial stability. This chapter will guide you through a detailed process of understanding your current financial obligations and responsibilities, determining the minimum income required for a smooth transition, and creating a comprehensive financial plan to ensure stability during this period.

1.1 Evaluating Personal Financial Obligations and Responsibilities

To begin, take a comprehensive look at your personal financial landscape. Start by identifying and listing all your recurring monthly expenses, including rent or mortgage payments, utilities, transportation costs, groceries, healthcare expenses, insurance premiums, loan repayments, and any other financial commitments. For example, if you are paying $1,500 in rent, $200 for utilities, $300 for groceries, and $150 for student loan repayments, your total monthly expenses would be $2,150.

Additionally, consider any outstanding debts, such as credit card balances, student loans, or personal loans. Take note of the minimum monthly payments required for each debt, as well as the total outstanding balances. For instance, if you have a credit card balance of $5,000 with a minimum monthly payment of $100, and a student loan with a monthly payment of $200 and a remaining balance of $10,000, your total debt obligations would be $300 per month.

1.2 Determining the Minimum Income Required

Once you have evaluated your financial obligations, it is time to determine the minimum income required to cover these expenses. Begin by categorising your expenses into fixed and variable costs. Fixed costs are those that remain relatively constant month after month, such as rent or mortgage payments, while variable costs may fluctuate based on your discretionary spending habits, such as entertainment or dining out.

Let's say your fixed monthly expenses amount to $1,700, which includes rent, utilities, and insurance premiums. Your variable expenses, such as groceries, transportation, and discretionary spending, average around $450 per month. This would give you a baseline figure of $2,150 as the minimum income required to sustain your essential lifestyle.

However, it's important to consider savings and emergency funds as part of your monthly commitments. Saving for emergencies and future goals is crucial for financial security. Let's say you aim to save $200 per month for your emergency fund and $300 per month for future investments. Including these savings commitments, your minimum income requirement would be $2,650 ($2,150 for essential expenses + $200 for emergency savings + $300 for future investments).

For more details about working out a proper personal financial plan, please refer to my other books on "Financial Freedom".

1.3 Creating a Comprehensive Financial Plan

With the minimum income requirement established, it is time to create a detailed financial plan. This plan will serve as a roadmap to help you navigate the transition while ensuring financial security.

To create your financial plan, you need to assess potential sources of income during the transition. For example, if you are currently employed and plan to continue working while starting your business, you can include your salary as a primary income source. Let's assume your monthly salary is $3,500.

Next, develop a monthly budget that aligns with your financial goals and the income you expect to earn during the transition. Allocate funds for your essential expenses, such as housing, utilities, transportation, groceries, and healthcare. For instance, if your essential expenses amount to $2,650 (as just explained), you can allocate this amount from your income.

Consider the costs associated with your business venture. Let's say you estimate that you will need an additional $500 per month for business-related expenses, such as website hosting, marketing materials, or software subscriptions. This would bring your total required budget to $3,150.

If your salary matches or exceeds your required budget, you are in a favourable position. You can allocate the surplus towards savings, emergency funds, or further investment in your business. However, if your salary falls short of the required budget, you need to explore alternative sources of income to bridge the gap. This could include taking on freelance work, finding part-time employment, or leveraging your savings.

By carefully evaluating your financial obligations, determining the minimum income required, and creating a comprehensive financial plan that includes savings and emergency funds, you can embark on your entrepreneurial journey with confidence and financial stability. This chapter equips you with the necessary tools and knowledge to maintain financial security during the transition while laying the groundwork for a successful and sustainable business.

EMPLOYED TO ENTREPRENEUR – Navigating The Transition With Financial Security & Business Success

CHAPTER II
IDENTIFYING THE RIGHT BUSINESS OPPORTUNITY

*I*n Chapter 2, we will embark on the exciting journey of identifying the right business opportunity that aligns with your skills, passions, and market demand. This chapter will provide you with a comprehensive understanding of the key considerations and steps involved in selecting a business opportunity that will set the stage for a successful transition from employment to entrepreneurship. Through detailed examples, you will gain practical insights and inspiration to make informed decisions.

Section 2.1: Exploring Business Ideas Aligned with Your Skills and Passions

1. **Assessing your skills and strengths:** To identify a business idea that resonates with you, it is crucial to assess your skills, strengths, and unique capabilities. Take inventory of your professional experiences, educational

7

background, and personal interests. Consider how these factors can be leveraged to create a business that showcases your expertise and fulfils your passions.

For example, if you have a background in marketing and a passion for health and wellness, you might consider starting a digital marketing agency specialising in promoting wellness products or services.

2. **Market demand and trends:** Researching market demand and trends is essential to identify viable business opportunities. Analyse industry reports, consumer behaviour, and emerging trends to understand the current and future needs of your target market. Look for gaps in the market that align with your skills and interests.

    For instance, with the rise of remote work and flexible lifestyles, you could explore business ideas related to remote productivity tools, co-working spaces, or digital nomad services.

Section 2.2: Assessing Profitability Potential and Scalability

1. **Financial viability:** Assessing the financial viability of a business opportunity is crucial to ensure its long-term sustainability. Conduct a thorough analysis of potential costs, revenue

streams, and profit margins. Consider factors such as initial investments, operational expenses, pricing strategies, and customer acquisition costs.

For example, if you are considering starting an e-commerce business, calculate the costs associated with inventory, website development, marketing, and shipping to determine the financial viability of your venture.

2. **Scalability and growth opportunities:** Evaluate the scalability and growth potential of the business opportunity. Consider if the market size allows for expansion, if there are opportunities to diversify your product or service offerings, or if there is potential for geographic expansion. Look for business models that can be replicated or scaled to accommodate growth.

For instance, a software-as-a-service (SaaS) business model offers scalability by providing a digital product that can be easily scaled to serve a growing customer base without significant increases in operational costs.

Section 2.3: Selecting a Business Model for the Transition Process

1. **Part-time or side business:** Starting a part-time or side business while maintaining employment provides a gradual transition into entrepreneurship. It allows you to test the market, build a customer base, and generate income while minimising the financial risks associated with leaving your job. Examples of part-time or side businesses include freelance consulting, online tutoring, or offering specialised services in your field of expertise.

    For instance, if you are a skilled graphic designer, you could offer freelance design services outside of your regular working hours to build your client base.

2. **Transitional business model:** A transitional business model involves offering services or products related to your expertise while simultaneously building your own business in the background. This approach allows you to leverage your existing skills, industry knowledge, and professional network while gradually transitioning into full-time entrepreneurship.

    For example, if you are a marketing professional, you could start by offering consulting services to clients while working on developing your own marketing agency.

Chapter 2 has provided you with an exploration

of identifying the right business opportunity. By assessing your skills and passions, researching market demand, evaluating financial viability, and considering scalability, you are well-equipped to make informed decisions. The examples presented throughout this chapter have showcased how individuals have successfully identified and pursued business opportunities. As you move forward, use this knowledge to find a business idea that aligns with your goals and paves the way for a successful transition from employment to entrepreneurship.

Just always make sure that you are working within the rules and contractual obligations of your current full-time job so that everything you do is above board.

CHAPTER III
CRAFTING A COMPREHENSIVE BUSINESS PLAN

*B*y setting clear goals, conducting thorough market research, and developing a detailed plan, you will lay a solid foundation for your transition from employment to full-time entrepreneurship. This chapter provides you with guidance and examples to help you create a robust business plan that addresses the challenges of the transition.

Section 3.1: Setting Clear Goals and Objectives for Your Business

1. **Defining your vision and mission:** To start, clearly articulate your vision for the business. Your vision represents your long-term aspirations and the impact you want to make. For example, if you're passionate about providing sustainable energy solutions, your vision could be to create a world where renewable energy is accessible to all.

Alongside your vision, develop a mission statement that outlines the specific objectives and values of your business. This statement will guide your decision-making and align your actions with your purpose.

2. **Establishing SMART goals:** Set SMART goals that are specific, measurable, attainable, relevant, and time-bound. These goals provide clarity and help you track your progress. For instance, if you're starting an e-commerce business selling handmade jewellery, a SMART goal could be to achieve $50,000 in sales within the first year of full-time entrepreneurship.

   Break down your goals into actionable steps to make them more achievable.

Section 3.2: Conducting Thorough Market Research and Defining Your Target Audience

1. **Market analysis:** Conduct a comprehensive market analysis to gain insights into the industry landscape, market trends, and competition. Identify key competitors, their products or services, pricing strategies, and target audience.

   For example, if you're planning to open a vegan bakery, research existing vegan bakeries in your area, their offerings, pricing, and customer reviews. Identify gaps in the market that you can capitalise on.

2. **Defining your target audience:** Define your target audience based on demographics, psychographics, and behaviour. Understand their needs, preferences, pain points, and buying habits. This information will help you tailor your products or services and develop effective marketing strategies.

    For instance, if you're starting a fitness app targeting busy professionals, your target audience might be men and women aged 25-40 who prioritise convenience and personalised workouts.

Section 3.3: Developing a Detailed Business Plan That Addresses the Transition

1. **Executive summary:** The executive summary provides an overview of your business plan, capturing the essence of your venture. It should include your business concept, target market, unique selling proposition, financial projections, and funding requirements. Write this section last, as it summarises the key elements of your plan.

2. **Company description and structure:** Describe your company, its legal structure, ownership, and management team. Highlight

your competitive advantage and what sets your
business apart.

For example, if you're starting a digital
marketing agency, emphasise the expertise and
experience of your team in delivering results-
driven campaigns.

3. **Products or services:** Provide a detailed
    description of your products or services,
    including their features, benefits, and how they
    address customer needs. Use examples to
    illustrate how your offerings solve specific
    problems or provide unique value. If you're
    offering personalised nutrition coaching,
    explain how your customised meal plans and
    ongoing support help clients achieve their
    health goals.

4. **Marketing and sales strategies:** Outline your
    marketing and sales strategies to reach and
    engage your target audience effectively. This
    includes your branding approach, advertising
    channels, pricing strategy, distribution
    channels, and customer acquisition tactics.

    For instance, if you're starting an online
    fashion boutique targeting fashion-forward
    millennials, describe how you will leverage
    social media platforms, influencer
    partnerships, and targeted online ads to build
    brand awareness and drive sales.

5. **Operations and management:** Detail your operational processes, including production or service delivery, quality control, inventory management, and customer service. Explain how you will manage day-to-day operations while transitioning from employment to full-time entrepreneurship. Provide examples of how you will optimise efficiency and ensure excellent customer experiences. If you're starting a subscription box service, describe your order fulfilment process, customer support protocols, and quality assurance measures.

6. **Financial projections and funding:** Present detailed financial projections, including income statements, cash flow statements, and balance sheets. Use realistic assumptions based on your market research and business model. Discuss your funding needs and potential sources of financing, such as personal savings, loans, or investors. Provide a timeline for when you expect to achieve profitability and how the transition from employment to full-time entrepreneurship will be financially supported.

Crafting a comprehensive business plan is a critical step in ensuring a smooth transition from employment to full-time entrepreneurship. By setting clear goals, conducting thorough market research, and developing a detailed plan, you

position yourself for success. The examples and
insights shared in this chapter serve as valuable
references to guide you through the process of
creating a robust business plan.

CHAPTER IV
BUILDING YOUR BUSINESS WHILE EMPLOYED

*B*alancing the demands of your job and your new venture requires careful time management and smart resource allocation. In this chapter, we will explore effective techniques for managing your time, outsourcing tasks, and leveraging flexible work arrangements to maximise your business growth.

Section 4.1: Managing Time Effectively Between Your Job And Business Responsibilities

1. **Prioritising tasks:** Identify high-impact tasks that contribute significantly to your business growth. For instance, if you're starting a graphic design business, prioritise tasks such as building a portfolio, networking with potential clients, and creating compelling proposals.

Example: Allocate specific time each week to work on developing your portfolio by creating design samples and showcasing your skills. Dedicate time for networking by attending industry events or reaching out to potential clients.

2. **Creating a schedule:** Develop a detailed schedule that includes dedicated time for both your job and your business. Allocate specific time blocks for business-related activities to ensure focused work without neglecting your job responsibilities.

   Example: Set aside two hours in the morning before work and two hours in the evening after work to focus on your business. During these time blocks, work on tasks like marketing research, client communication, and business planning.

3. **Time blocking:** Implement time blocking techniques to optimise productivity. Assign specific time slots for different types of tasks to avoid multitasking and maintain focus.

   Example: Dedicate a time block each day for market research and competitor analysis. Another time block can be allocated for content creation and updating your website.

Section 4.2: Outsourcing or Delegating Tasks To Maximise Productivity

1. **Identifying tasks suitable for outsourcing:** Evaluate your business tasks and identify areas where external expertise can be leveraged. Tasks like administrative work, graphic design, or social media management can often be effectively outsourced.

   Example: If you lack graphic design skills, consider outsourcing tasks such as logo design or website development to a skilled freelancer. This allows you to focus on core business activities while ensuring professional design work.

2. **Finding and hiring reliable help:** Research freelancers, agencies, or virtual assistants specialising in the tasks you want to outsource. Utilise online platforms like Upwork or Fiverr to find qualified professionals. Conduct interviews, check references, and review portfolios to ensure you hire reliable and competent individuals.

   Example: If you need assistance with social media management, search for experienced social media managers on freelance platforms. Interview candidates, review their past work, and select someone who aligns with your business goals and communication style.

3. **Delegating effectively:** If you have team members or employees, delegate tasks to them to maximise productivity. Clearly communicate expectations, provide necessary resources, and offer guidance to ensure tasks are completed satisfactorily. Regularly communicate with your team to track progress and provide feedback.

   Example: If you have an employee who excels at content writing, delegate blog writing tasks to them. Provide clear guidelines and expectations, review their work, and offer constructive feedback to ensure quality output.

Section 4.3: Leveraging Weekends, Evenings, and Flexible Work Arrangements

1. **Utilising weekends and evenings:** Make the most of your weekends and evenings by dedicating focused blocks of time to your business. Use these periods for tasks that require concentration and strategic thinking, such as developing marketing campaigns, creating content, or working on long-term business planning.

   Example: Allocate a significant portion of your weekends to conducting market research, analysing competitors, and developing a comprehensive marketing strategy. In the evenings, focus on content creation, updating your website, or engaging with potential clients on social media.

2. **Flexible work arrangements:** Explore flexible work arrangements with your employer to create more time for your business. Negotiate options such as reduced hours, remote work, or flexible scheduling that allow you to allocate specific time blocks during the workweek for your business-related activities. Ensure that you continue to fulfil your job responsibilities effectively.

    Example: If your employer offers remote work options, negotiate to work from home one or two days a week. This allows you to dedicate those days entirely to your business while still fulfilling your job duties on the other days.

3. **Creating boundaries:** Maintain a healthy work-life balance by setting clear boundaries between your job and your business. Communicate your availability to both your employer and your clients or customers, and establish guidelines for response times. By setting expectations and boundaries, you can avoid burnout and maintain focus on your business goals.

    Example: Clearly communicate to your clients that you respond to business-related inquiries within 24-48 hours and provide specific hours during which you're available for client meetings or calls. Inform your employer about your preferred communication channels and times when you can be reached for work-related matters.

Building a business while employed requires effective time management, outsourcing or delegating tasks, and leveraging flexible work arrangements. By managing your time efficiently, outsourcing non-core tasks, and utilising flexible work options, you can effectively grow your business while maintaining your employment. Remember to maintain a healthy work-life balance and remain focused on your long-term business goals.

CHAPTER V
FINANCIAL PLANNING AND RISK MANAGEMENT

C hapter 5 explores the crucial aspects of financial planning and risk management when transitioning from employment to full involvement in your business. It highlights the importance of assessing the financial impact, creating a budget, managing cash flow, and implementing strategies to mitigate risks. By understanding these principles, you can maintain financial stability and minimise potential setbacks.

Section 5.1: Assessing The Financial Impact of Transitioning

1. **Evaluating current and future financial obligations:** Review your current financial commitments, including monthly expenses, loan repayments, and savings goals. Consider how transitioning to full-time entrepreneurship may impact your income, expenses, and long-term financial goals.

Example: Calculate your current monthly expenses, such as rent/mortgage, utilities, groceries, transportation, and healthcare. Assess how these expenses may change when you no longer have a steady paycheck and need to allocate funds for business-related costs.

2. **Estimating income potential:** Research and estimate the income potential of your business based on market trends, competition, and your pricing strategy. Be realistic and consider both short-term and long-term revenue projections.

Example: If you plan to offer consulting services, research the average rates in your industry and estimate the number of clients you can reasonably acquire in the initial months. Calculate the projected income based on these factors.

3. **Projecting expenses:** Identify and estimate the expenses associated with your business, including equipment, marketing, inventory, and professional services. Account for both one-time startup costs and recurring expenses.

Example: List the essential business expenses, such as website development, marketing materials, software subscriptions, and professional fees. Research the market rates and estimate the costs associated with each item.

Section 5.2: Creating A Budget And Managing Cash Flow

1. **Developing a comprehensive budget:** Create a detailed budget that encompasses both personal and business expenses. Allocate funds for essential living expenses, business-related costs, savings, and emergency funds.

    Example: Divide your budget into categories such as housing, transportation, groceries, business operations, marketing, and savings. Set realistic limits for each category and track your actual spending regularly.

2. **Managing personal and business cash flow:** Implement strategies to manage cash flow effectively. Separate your personal and business finances, track income and expenses meticulously, and ensure you have sufficient funds for both personal and business needs.

    Example: Open separate bank accounts for personal and business finances. Regularly monitor your income and expenses using accounting software or spreadsheets. Prioritise essential personal expenses and allocate the remaining funds for business-related costs.

3. **Building an emergency fund:** Create an emergency fund to provide a financial safety net in case of unexpected expenses or business challenges. Aim to save three to six months'

worth of living expenses to handle any contingencies.

Example: Set aside a portion of your income each month specifically for your emergency fund. Automate the savings process by transferring a fixed amount to a separate savings account regularly.

Section 5.3: Mitigating Risks Through Insurance, Contingency Planning, And Savings Strategies

1. **Insurance coverage:** Evaluate the insurance coverage necessary for your business and personal life. Consider options such as liability insurance, professional indemnity insurance, health insurance, and disability insurance to protect yourself and your business.

   Example: If you offer professional services, explore professional liability insurance to safeguard against potential legal claims. Research and compare insurance providers to find suitable coverage at a reasonable cost.

2. **Contingency planning:** Develop a contingency plan to address potential risks and challenges that may arise during the transition phase. Identify alternative income sources, explore partnerships or collaborations, and create backup plans to mitigate risks.

Example: If your business heavily relies on a single client or revenue stream, explore diversification options. Identify potential clients or additional income streams that can support your business in case of any disruptions.

3. **Savings strategies:** Implement savings strategies to build a financial buffer and support your business during the transition. Set aside funds for future investments, business growth, and personal financial goals.

    Example: Allocate a portion of your income specifically for business savings. Determine a percentage or fixed amount that you can consistently save each month to support your business expansion plans or handle unexpected expenses.

Financial planning and risk management are vital components of transitioning from employment to full involvement in your business. By assessing the financial impact, creating a budget, managing cash flow, and implementing strategies to mitigate risks, you can navigate the transition period with greater financial security and resilience. Remember to regularly review and adjust your financial plans as your business evolves.

CHAPTER VI
LEVERAGING YOUR EMPLOYMENT FOR BUSINESS SUCCESS

We now explore how you can utilise your job's resources, network, and expertise to propel your entrepreneurial venture forward. By recognising and capitalising on these opportunities, you can navigate the transition more smoothly and enhance your business growth prospects.

Section 6.1: Utilising Your Current Job's Resources

1. **Accessing physical resources:** Identify and utilise the physical resources available through your current job, such as office space, equipment, technology, and tools. Leverage these resources to minimise your initial business setup costs. Just make sure that your employer allows you to use these resources for the purposes you intend to use them for.

31

Example: If your employer allows it, utilise office space during non-working hours for business meetings or as a temporary workspace. Utilise company-owned equipment and technology for certain business tasks, reducing the need for immediate investments.

2. **Tapping into intellectual resources:** Leverage the expertise and knowledge available within your workplace. Engage in conversations with colleagues or superiors who possess relevant industry experience and seek their guidance and advice.

    Example: If you work in a marketing department, consult with colleagues who have expertise in digital marketing or branding to gain insights for your own business. Engage in discussions and actively participate in knowledge-sharing opportunities within your organisation.

3. **Utilising professional development opportunities:** Take advantage of professional development programmes or training offered by your employer. Enhance your skills and acquire knowledge that can directly benefit your business.

    Example: Attend workshops, seminars, or webinars organised by your employer to gain new insights into areas relevant to your business. Apply the knowledge you acquire to improve your business strategies and operations.

Section 6.2: Exploring Collaborative Opportunities

1. **Collaboration with colleagues:** Identify potential collaboration opportunities with colleagues who share similar interests or complementary skills. Pooling resources and expertise can lead to mutually beneficial partnerships that accelerate business growth.

    Example: If you're a graphic designer starting your own design agency, collaborate with a colleague who specialises in copywriting to offer comprehensive design and content services to clients.

2. **Collaborative projects with your employer:** Explore projects or initiatives within your current organisation that align with your entrepreneurial goals. Propose collaboration ideas that can benefit both your employer and your business.

    Example: If your employer is planning a marketing campaign, offer to contribute your expertise and insights. This allows you to showcase your skills while also promoting your own business to a wider audience.

3. **Joint ventures or partnerships:** Consider partnering with your employer or colleagues to create joint ventures or strategic partnerships. By combining resources and expertise, you can enhance your business's capabilities and market reach.

   Example: If you're a software developer, collaborate with your employer to develop a new software product that can be marketed and sold jointly. This allows you to leverage your employer's brand and customer base for mutual growth.

Section 6.3: Leveraging Your Employer's Support

1. **Communicating your entrepreneurial goals:** Openly communicate your entrepreneurial aspirations with your employer, ensuring they are aware of your long-term plans. Seek their support and understanding, emphasising how your business can complement your current role.

   Example: Schedule a meeting with your supervisor or human resources department to discuss your entrepreneurial journey. Explain how your business aligns with your skills and interests, and highlight the potential benefits it can bring to your employer.

2. **Flexible work arrangements:** Explore the possibility of flexible work arrangements that allow you to allocate dedicated time for your business while fulfilling your job responsibilities. Negotiate options such as reduced hours, remote work, or flexible scheduling.

   Example: Propose a flexible work schedule that allows you to dedicate specific days or hours to focus solely on your business activities. This arrangement can provide you with the necessary time and flexibility to nurture your entrepreneurial venture.

3. **Employer support programmes:** Inquire about any support programmes or resources offered by your employer for employees pursuing entrepreneurial endeavours. Some companies provide mentorship programmes, financial assistance, or access to business networks.

   Example: Take advantage of mentorship programmes where experienced entrepreneurs within your organisation can guide you through the challenges of starting your own business. Tap into available resources and support networks to gain insights and connections.

Leveraging your current employment for business success is a strategic approach to navigate the transition from employee to entrepreneur. By utilising your job's resources, exploring collaborative opportunities, and seeking your employer's support, you can enhance your business's growth potential and increase your chances of a smooth and successful transition.

CHAPTER VII
MARKETING AND SALES STRATEGIES FOR TRANSITIONING ENTREPRENEURS

*N*ow, let's explore how to develop a targeted marketing plan, leverage online platforms and automation tools, and implement effective sales techniques to generate income and attract customers during this critical period.

Section 7.1: Developing A Targeted Marketing Plan

1. **Defining your target audience:** Identify and define your target audience based on demographics, interests, and needs. Understand their pain points and motivations to tailor your marketing messages effectively.

   Example: If you're starting a fitness coaching business targeting busy professionals, your target audience may be working individuals aged 25-40 who seek convenient and efficient workout solutions to fit their hectic schedules.

2. **Crafting a compelling value proposition:** Develop a clear and concise value proposition that highlights the unique benefits and solutions your business offers. Clearly communicate why customers should choose your product or service over competitors.

   Example: If you're offering a meal delivery service focusing on healthy and customised meals, your value proposition could be: "Enjoy nutritious, chef-prepared meals delivered to your doorstep, tailored to your dietary preferences and wellness goals."

3. **Choosing effective marketing channels:** Identify the most suitable marketing channels to reach your target audience. Consider online platforms, social media, email marketing, content marketing, and offline methods, based on your audience's preferences and behaviour.

   Example: If your target audience consists of tech-savvy individuals, invest in online channels such as social media advertising, influencer partnerships, and content marketing through blogs or videos.

Section 7.2: Utilising Online Platforms And Automation Tools

1. **Building an online presence:** Create a professional website that showcases your brand, products, and services. Optimise it for search engines to increase visibility. Establish social media profiles on platforms where your target audience is most active.

   Example: Develop a website that features compelling visuals, engaging content, and clear calls-to-action. Establish a presence on social media platforms like Facebook, Instagram, or LinkedIn to connect with potential customers and share valuable content.

2. **Implementing content marketing:** Create informative and valuable content that educates and engages your audience. Share blog posts, articles, videos, or podcasts that align with your target audience's interests and challenges.

   Example: If you're running a fashion consultancy business, create blog posts or videos providing style tips, outfit inspirations, and wardrobe organisation advice. Demonstrate your expertise and build trust with your audience.

3. **Leveraging automation tools:** Utilise automation tools and software to streamline your marketing processes, save time, and increase efficiency. Automate email marketing,

social media scheduling, customer relationship management (CRM), and analytics.

Example: Use email marketing software to automate personalised email campaigns that nurture leads and convert them into customers. Schedule social media posts in advance using tools like Hootsuite or Buffer to maintain a consistent online presence.

Section 7.3: Implementing Sales Techniques

1. **Creating a sales funnel:** Design a sales funnel that guides potential customers through each stage of the buying journey. Develop strategies to capture leads, nurture them, and convert them into paying customers.

   Example: Build a sales funnel by offering a free ebook or a discount coupon in exchange for email sign-ups. Nurture leads with valuable content and personalised email sequences, ultimately leading them to make a purchase.

2. **Offering limited-time promotions or incentives:** Create a sense of urgency and incentivise purchases by offering limited-time promotions, discounts, or bonuses. This can help generate immediate income during the transition phase.

   Example: Offer a limited-time discount for new customers or create bundle packages that provide additional value for a limited period. Promote these offers through targeted marketing campaigns to drive sales.

3. **Building customer relationships:** Focus on building strong relationships with your customers through personalised communication, exceptional customer service, and follow-up strategies. Repeat customers can become valuable brand advocates and provide referrals.

   Example: Implement customer relationship management (CRM) tools to track customer interactions and preferences. Send personalised thank-you emails, offer loyalty rewards, and actively seek feedback to strengthen relationships.

In Chapter 7, you explored the essential aspects of marketing and sales strategies for transitioning entrepreneurs. By developing a targeted marketing plan, leveraging online platforms and automation tools, and implementing effective sales techniques, you can generate income, attract customers, and establish a solid foundation for your business during the transition phase.

CHAPTER VIII
BUILDING A SUPPORTIVE NETWORK

*T*his chapter explores strategies for seeking guidance from mentors and fellow entrepreneurs, joining entrepreneurial communities, and cultivating relationships with supportive colleagues, friends, and fellow entrepreneurs.

Section 8.1: Seeking Guidance From Mentors And Fellow Entrepreneurs

1. **Identifying potential mentors:** Identify experienced individuals who have successfully navigated the transition from employment to entrepreneurship. Seek mentors who can provide guidance, advice, and valuable insights based on their own experiences.

   Example: Look for mentors through networking events, industry associations, or online platforms dedicated to mentorship

programmes. Consider reaching out to
successful entrepreneurs in your field and
expressing your interest in learning from them.

2. **Building relationships with mentors:**
    Establish a meaningful connection with your
    mentors by demonstrating your commitment,
    willingness to learn, and respect for their time.
    Maintain regular communication, seek their
    guidance on specific challenges, and show
    appreciation for their support.

    Example: Schedule periodic meetings or virtual
    sessions with your mentors to discuss your
    progress, seek advice on critical decisions, and
    gain insights into the entrepreneurial journey.
    Be proactive in implementing their
    recommendations and providing updates on
    your achievements.

Section 8.2: Joining Entrepreneurial Communities and Attending Industry-Specific Events

1. **Identifying relevant entrepreneurial
    communities:** Research and join
    entrepreneurial communities and forums
    where you can connect with like-minded
    individuals, share experiences, and exchange
    knowledge. Look for communities specific to
    your industry or general entrepreneurship.

Example: Explore online platforms like LinkedIn Groups, industry-specific forums, or local entrepreneurship meetups. Engage in discussions, ask questions, and contribute your expertise to build valuable connections.

2. **Attending industry-specific events:** Participate in industry conferences, workshops, seminars, and networking events to expand your network, learn from industry experts, and stay updated on emerging trends. These events provide opportunities for meaningful connections and potential collaboration.

Example: Attend conferences or trade shows related to your business niche or attend workshops and seminars on topics such as marketing, technology, or business growth. Actively engage with other attendees, exchange business cards, and follow up with potential contacts.

Section 8.3: Cultivating Relationships with Supportive Colleagues, Friends, and Fellow Entrepreneurs

1. **Engaging with supportive colleagues:** Build relationships with colleagues who understand and support your entrepreneurial aspirations. Seek their advice, share your

progress, and leverage their expertise or
connections whenever appropriate.

Example: Identify colleagues who have an
entrepreneurial mindset or are supportive of
your goals. Arrange informal meetings or lunch
breaks to discuss business ideas, seek feedback,
or brainstorm solutions. Offer your support in
return and celebrate each other's successes.

2. **Building connections with friends and
   fellow entrepreneurs:** Expand your network
   by connecting with friends who are also
   pursuing entrepreneurial ventures or have
   experience in relevant industries. Share
   insights, exchange resources, and provide
   mutual support throughout your journeys.

   Example: Attend local startup events,
   entrepreneurship workshops, or industry-
   specific gatherings where you can meet other
   entrepreneurs. Nurture relationships with
   individuals who share similar goals and values,
   and regularly engage in conversations and
   collaboration.

Chapter 8 highlighted the significance of
building a supportive network as an employed
entrepreneur. By seeking guidance from mentors
and fellow entrepreneurs, joining entrepreneurial
communities, and cultivating relationships with
colleagues, friends, and fellow entrepreneurs, you

can gain valuable insights, find support during challenges, and create a community of like-minded individuals to propel your entrepreneurial journey forward.

CHAPTER IX
SCALING YOUR BUSINESS AND FULL-TIME ENTREPRENEURSHIP

*S*caling your business and transitioning from employment to full-time entrepreneurship is a critical phase. It focuses on determining the right time to make the transition, planning for financial stability, and implementing strategies to scale your business and optimise income generation.

Section 9.1: Knowing When It's the Right Time to Transition

1. **Assessing business readiness:** Evaluate the growth and stability of your business, considering factors such as revenue, customer base, market demand, and operational efficiency. Determine if your business can sustain your financial needs and provide a solid foundation for full-time entrepreneurship.

Example: Analyse key performance indicators (KPIs) such as sales growth, profit margins, customer retention rates, and market trends. Consider seeking the advice of mentors or industry experts to gain an objective perspective on your business's readiness for full-time entrepreneurship.

2. **Evaluating personal financial stability:** Assess your personal financial situation and ensure you have a sufficient financial cushion to support yourself during the transition period. Consider factors such as savings, emergency funds, debt obligations, and monthly expenses.

Example: Create a comprehensive personal budget that accounts for your living expenses, business costs, and any additional financial commitments. Evaluate your savings and emergency funds to determine if they can sustain you during the transition phase when income may fluctuate.

Section 9.2: Planning the Final Shift and Ensuring Financial Stability

1. **Creating a transition plan:** Develop a detailed plan outlining the steps and timeline for transitioning from employment to full-time entrepreneurship. Consider factors such as completing ongoing work commitments,

notifying employers, and ensuring a smooth handover of responsibilities.

Example: Create a timeline that outlines specific milestones and tasks leading up to your final shift. Break down the necessary actions, such as completing pending projects, notifying employers of your intention to leave, and securing necessary licenses or permits for your business.

2. **Establishing financial stability:** Implement strategies to ensure financial stability during the transition phase and beyond. This may include maintaining a cash reserve, diversifying income sources, and exploring alternative funding options.

Example: Set aside a portion of your income specifically for business and personal expenses during the transition phase. Explore options for securing additional funding, such as small business loans, crowdfunding, or seeking investment from partners or stakeholders.

Section 9.3: Strategies for Scaling Your Business and Optimising Income Generation

1. **Expanding your customer base:** Focus on acquiring new customers and expanding your reach through targeted marketing campaigns, partnerships, and referral programmes.

Implement strategies to increase brand visibility and generate a steady stream of leads.

Example: Develop a comprehensive marketing plan that includes digital marketing strategies, social media advertising, content marketing, and referral incentives. Collaborate with complementary businesses to cross-promote each other's products or services.

2. **Streamlining operations and maximising efficiency:** Optimise your business operations to improve productivity, reduce costs, and increase profitability. Identify areas where you can automate processes, outsource tasks, or adopt technology solutions to streamline operations.

Example: Evaluate your business processes and identify opportunities for automation or outsourcing. Utilise project management tools, cloud-based systems, or virtual assistants to streamline administrative tasks and free up time for strategic activities.

Chapter 9 delved into the crucial phase of scaling your business and transitioning to full-time entrepreneurship. By assessing business readiness, planning the final shift, ensuring financial stability, and implementing strategies to scale your business and optimise income generation, you can lay the

foundation for sustainable growth and success as a
full-time entrepreneur.

CHAPTER X
EMBRACING FULL-TIME ENTREPRENEURSHIP

*E*xploring the emotional and practical aspects of embracing full-time entrepreneurship is quite important. Let's now address the challenges of leaving employment behind, building a routine and structure for your entrepreneurial journey, and continuing to prioritise financial stability and long-term business growth.

Section 10.1: Navigating the Emotional Aspects of Leaving Employment

1. **Managing fear and uncertainty:** Acknowledge and address the fears and uncertainties that may arise when leaving the security of employment. Develop strategies to manage stress, build resilience, and maintain a positive mindset throughout the transition.

Example: Engage in activities that promote mental and emotional well-being, such as meditation, exercise, journaling, or seeking support from a therapist or support group. Surround yourself with positive influences and seek inspiration from successful entrepreneurs who have gone through similar transitions.

2. **Overcoming the fear of failure:** Recognise that failure is a natural part of the entrepreneurial journey and an opportunity for growth. Embrace a mindset that views failure as a steppingstone toward success and a valuable learning experience.

Example: Reframe your perspective on failure by focusing on the lessons learned and the resilience gained from challenging experiences. Surround yourself with a supportive network that encourages experimentation, risk-taking, and learning from mistakes.

Section 10.2: Building a Routine and Structure for Your Entrepreneurial Journey

1. **Establishing a daily routine:** Create a structured daily routine that allows you to balance your business responsibilities, personal well-being, and other commitments. Define specific time blocks for core business activities, personal development, and self-care.

Example: Designate dedicated blocks of time for focused work on your business, such as strategic planning, product development, or client acquisition. Schedule regular breaks for rest, exercise, and personal time to maintain a healthy work-life balance.

2. **Setting goals and milestones:** Set clear and achievable goals for your business and establish milestones to track your progress. Break down larger goals into smaller, actionable steps to maintain motivation and measure success.

   Example: Use the SMART goal framework (specific, measurable, achievable, relevant, and time-bound) to define goals that align with your vision. Regularly review and update your goals, and celebrate milestones along the way to stay motivated and engaged.

Section 10.3: Prioritising Financial Stability and Long-Term Business Growth

1. **Managing finances effectively:** Continue to prioritise financial stability by monitoring cash flow, tracking expenses, and adjusting your budget as needed. Implement strategies to optimise revenue generation and maximise profitability.

   Example: Use financial management tools or software to track income and expenses, maintain accurate records, and generate financial reports. Regularly review your business finances and make informed decisions based on financial data and projections.

2. **Investing in long-term business growth:** Allocate resources to activities that support long-term business growth, such as marketing, research and development, and talent acquisition. Continuously seek opportunities to innovate, expand your market reach, and stay ahead of industry trends.

Example: Allocate a portion of your revenue or profits to marketing initiatives, product or service enhancements, and professional development. Stay informed about industry trends, emerging technologies, and customer needs to adapt your business strategy accordingly.

Chapter 10 emphasised the significance of embracing full-time entrepreneurship and provided guidance on navigating the emotional aspects, building a routine and structure, and prioritising financial stability and long-term business growth. By addressing these key factors, you can confidently embark on your full-time entrepreneurial journey and set yourself up for sustainable success.

SUMMARY AND CONCLUSION

*C*ongratulations on reaching the end of "Employed To Entrepreneur: Navigating The Transition With Financial Security & Business Success." Throughout this book, we've explored valuable insights and strategies to help you transition from employment to full-time entrepreneurship while maintaining financial stability. Let's briefly recap the key takeaways from our journey.

We began by recognising the advantages of maintaining employment while pursuing entrepreneurship and emphasised the importance of striking a balance between your job and business endeavours.

Assessing your financial stability is crucial before making the transition. Evaluate your personal financial obligations, determine the minimum income required, and create a comprehensive financial plan to ensure a solid foundation during the shift.

Identifying the right business opportunity is essential. Explore ideas aligned with your skills, passions, and market demand. Assess their profitability potential and scalability, and choose a business model that accommodates the transition process.

Crafting a comprehensive business plan is your roadmap to success. Set clear goals, conduct thorough market research, and develop a detailed plan that addresses the transition from employment to full-time entrepreneurship.

Building your business while employed necessitates effective time management. Delegate tasks or outsource when necessary to maximise productivity. Leverage weekends, evenings, and flexible work arrangements to focus on business growth.

Financial planning and risk management are vital. Assess the financial impact of transitioning, create a budget, manage cash flow, and mitigate risks through insurance, contingency planning, and savings strategies.

Leveraging your employment for business success involves utilizing your job's resources, network, and expertise. Explore collaborative opportunities with your employer or colleagues, and seek their support during the transition.

Marketing and sales strategies tailored to transitioning entrepreneurs are crucial for generating income. Develop a targeted marketing plan, leverage online platforms and automation tools, and implement effective sales techniques.

Building a supportive network of mentors, fellow entrepreneurs, and like-minded individuals provides guidance and inspiration. Seek their guidance, join entrepreneurial communities, and cultivate relationships with supportive colleagues and friends.

Scaling your business and making the final shift to full-time entrepreneurship require careful planning and timing. Implement strategies to optimise income generation and ensure financial stability.

Embracing full-time entrepreneurship involves navigating the emotional and practical aspects of leaving employment behind. Build a routine and structure for your entrepreneurial journey while prioritising financial stability and long-term business growth.

In conclusion, transitioning from employment to entrepreneurship requires careful planning, resilience, and determination. By embracing the advantages of your employment, setting clear goals, conducting thorough research, and leveraging support networks, you can successfully navigate the transition while maintaining financial security and achieving business success.

Now, armed with the knowledge and strategies shared in this book, it's time for you to embark on your entrepreneurial adventure. Believe in yourself, stay focused, and remember that success comes through consistent action and a growth mindset. Embrace the advantages of your employment, harness your skills and passion, and build a business

that not only provides financial security but also
fulfils your entrepreneurial dreams.

Best of luck on your journey!

Hassan Afifi

ABOUT THE AUTHOR

Hassan Afifi is a UK-based investment professional. He started investing and trading in financial markets in the early 1990s while at university. He holds a BA in economics.

Hassan has worked in institutional equity sales, advising some of the world's largest fund managers on their investments across different geographies and sectors.

He has also worked in corporate finance, helping entrepreneurs start or grow their businesses, raise funds for their projects, and guide management teams through their financial planning processes.

Hassan returned to the investment world full-time in 2020 focusing on wealth management to try and help as many people as he can to achieve their financial freedom.

www.ingramcontent.com/pod-product-compliance
Lightning Source LLC
Chambersburg PA
CBHW070457220526
45466CB00004B/1862